The Hitler Albums

The Hitler Albums

MUSSOLINI'S STATE VISIT TO GERMANY
SEPTEMBER 25 - 29, 1937

1st EDITION

COPYRIGHT ©1970 BY

ROGER JAMES BENDER
AND
DAVID F. FASOLD

ISBN No. 0-912138-04-1

PRINTED IN THE UNITED STATES OF AMERICA
BY
D-D ASSOC., PALO ALTO, CALIFORNIA

DESIGNED AND ILLUSTRATED
BY
ROGER JAMES BENDER

R. JAMES BENDER PUBLISHING P.O. BOX 1425, MOUNTAIN VIEW, CALIFORNIA 94040

Preface

 The significance and ramifications of Mussolini's state visit to Germany in September 1937 have long been obscured by the maze of modern European events. This German spectacle of power, as witnessed by the Duce during his visit, intoxicated him to the point of permanently falling under the influence of Hitler. The trip to Germany also led to a return visit by Hitler to Italy in 1938 at which time the seeds for a "Pact of Steel" were sown. This pact, which was to come into reality a year and a half later, would unite the two nations in a common cause and lead them down the road of aggression to their eventual destruction.

This author considered it an honour when the two Hitler albums were brought to him for inspection by their present owner. One was a complete photographic study of Mussolini's state visit to Germany in September 1937 and the other was of Hitler's return visit to Italy in May 1938. Further research into their authenticity revealed that they had been compiled by Geno Mele, with the aid of Heinrich Hoffmann's staff, at the Istituto Nazionale Luce. A total of fifteen such sets were produced, one in brown leather covers for Hitler and the remainder in blue canvas-type covers for the Duce and his ministers. Hitler's set was presented to him in late May of 1938.

ISTITUTO NAZIONALE LUCE

IL VIAGGIO DEL DUCE
IN GERMANIA

24 - 30 Settembre Anno XV° dell' E. F.

Omaggio del Marchese
G. PAULUCCI DI CALBOLI BARONE
Presidente dell' Istituto Nazionale LUCE

COVER OF THE ORIGINAL "VISIT TO GERMANY" ALBUM.

On May 6, 1945, Hitler's "Berghof Obersalzberg" was occupied by the 506th Parachute Regiment of the 101st Airborne Division. As the souvenir hunters from this unit roamed the grounds searching for reminders of their stay, one sergeant entered Hitler's library and noticed the two magnificent, leather bound albums on a shelf. He quickly commandeered them and brought them back to the United States in July 1945 where they had remained in obscurity until their discovery by the present owner in 1968.

It should be noted that several photos from other sources have been added to the originals from the "visit to Germany" album. This was done to create a complete photographic sequence which would complement the sequence of the text. This procedure will be repeated in the production of "The Hitler Albums" (Hitler's state visit to Italy, May 4-9, 1938) which will be published later this year.

Now! . . . Prepare to experience the most dynamic spectacle of power ever witnessed in the Third Reich . . . in its parades, maneuvers, tours and demonstrations, just as the Duce did . . . thirty-three years ago.

Acknowledgements

I would like to thank the following for their kind and generous assistance in the production of this book: Rudy A. D'Angelo, David F. Fasold, Walter H. Kopp, Guenther G. Schoen, Jerry Weiblen and The Hoover Library staff at Stanford University.

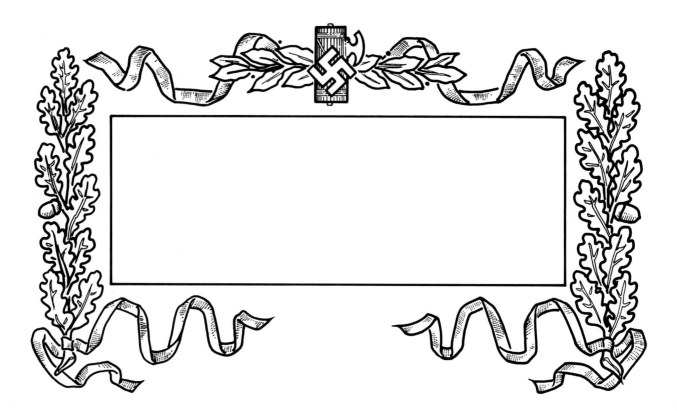

Historical Background

Hitler stated, in his writings from "Mein Kampf," that it would be an advantage for Germany to improve relations with Italy in the future. The pursuit of this policy was not possible after his ascension to power, however, due to one major stumbling block — Hitler's own birthplace of Austria. This small country, which was the last fragment of the Hapsburg empire, had been granted independence by the peacemakers of 1919. It was Italy's prime guarantee of security as it served as a buffer between her and Europe. For this reason Italy could not allow Austria to be absorbed into Germany or fall under German control.

In 1934, civil war broke out between the Austrian Clericals and the Austrian Socialists. These hostilities in turn stirred up the Austrian Nazis. They were encouraged by Munich radio and received money and equipment from Germany. German diplomats, hoping that Hitler would not actively push the Austrian question, arranged a meeting between Hitler and Mussolini at Venice on June 14, 1934. They believed that by meeting Mussolini face to face, Hitler could be pushed into concession. At this meeting, Hitler and Mussolini pronounced their mutual dislike of France and the Soviet Union and Hitler renounced any desire to annex Austria. The Duce requested that the Austrian Nazis drop their terroristic campaign, and in turn Dollfuss, the Clerical Chancellor, would treat them more sympathetically. Hitler, however, did nothing to fulfill Mussolini's demand and on July 25 the Nazis of Vienna occupied the Chancellery, murdered Dollfuss and attempted to seize power. At this critical moment, Mussolini made his first major bid as an international leader. He mobilized Italy's crack mountain regiments in the mountain gorges leading to the Brenner Pass, threatening to beat any German force into Austria if necessary.[1] Thus, Hitler could do nothing to help his Austrian adherents and stood helplessly by while Schuschnigg, successor to Dollfuss, restored order under Mussolini's protection.

For years the Duce had preached the right of might and promised to restore the Roman Empire as well as the grandeur of Rome. The

---

1. This gesture was sufficient to halt the German plans for the absorption of Austria. It should be noted that Mussolini was very disappointed that the Western Powers had stood aside and failed to support Italy. He later remarked to his wife, "I expected more from our Western friends, Rachele. They've let me down. Their apathy could have been disastrous." Rachele Mussolini, *My Life with Mussolini* (London: Robert Hale Limited, 1959), p. 81.

"garden of Africa," Abyssinia, was the first to feel his might. In October 1935, Italian armies plunged into the small country from three directions. Italy soon became isolated by world opinion and threatened by the League of Nations with economic sanctions. Hitler carefully watched the Abyssinian conflict and the moves of the splitting Western powers. He felt that a victorious Italy promised to be a worthy ally as she continued her advances against Abyssinia. Hitler therefore offered military assistance to Italy as soon as Germany's rearming program allowed it. The war ended before any formal commitments were ever made. Hitler then offered to recognize the newly enlarged Italian Empire, which cost him nothing and greatly pleased Mussolini who was presently enraged at the majority of European countries for refusing him recognition.

On July 11, 1936, the final stumbling block between close German-Italian relations was eliminated by the "Gentleman's Agreement." In this agreement, Hitler recognized the full sovereignty of Austria and in return Schuschnigg acknowledged that Austria was a "German State," agreed to admit members of the so-called "National Opposition" into his government and gave amnesty to Nazi political prisoners in Austria.

The birth of the Rome-Berlin Axis was now imminent as Italy's relations with France and England had been severely strained by the opposing interests brought about by the Abyssinian conflict. The advisability of standing shoulder to shoulder with Germany and confronting the Western powers was clear.

In the shaping of the Axis, Galeazzo Ciano[2] went to Germany where he met Hitler and Joachim von Ribbentrop, the Führer's special advisor on foreign policy. At this and subsequent meetings at Berchtesgaden, five points were worked out in the collaboration between the two countries and viewpoints of both dictators were carefully examined. Ciano's reports of the meetings were found satisfactory and on November 1, 1936, Mussolini publicly announced a German-Italian agreement which constituted an "Axis" — around which the other European powers might work together. Despite the Axis and the repeated mutual professions of friendship, however, the relations between the two leaders remained strained with certain suspicions. They watched each other's diplomatic activities with Great Britain and also the pressures each exerted over Austria.

In September 1936, German Minister of Justice, Hans Frank conveyed to the Duce, "The Führer desires to receive you in Germany at the earliest possible moment, not only in your capacity as head of the

---

2. Ciano was Mussolini's brother-in-law and Italian Minister of Foreign Affairs.

government but also as founder and Duce of a party with affinities to National Socialism." Mussolini expressed his wishes to undertake the trip, "It must, however, be well prepared so as to produce concrete results. It will cause a great stir and must therefore be historically important in its results."[3] The Duce was anxious to prove that he could excite a Berlin crowd to the same heights of enthusiasm as he had done in Rome. Count Ciano personally made the plans for the state visit which was scheduled from September 25-29, 1937. He emphasized the importance of uniforms, "We must appear more Prussian than the Prussians."

As Mussolini boarded the train in Rome on September 24, he wore a splendid uniform specially designed for the occasion, a grey-blue Corporal of Honour uniform with a cornflower blue sash across his chest and a black militia cap adorned with a red cord. His staff, which consisted of Ciano, Alfieri, the Minister of Press and Propaganda, Storace, the Party secretary and about 100 officials, journalists and subordinates, also were bedecked in finery. From Rome, Mussolini's train stopped at Forli where he paused for family kisses and well-wishes. His special nine-coach armoured train then chugged on to its historic journey. When the train pulled into the Alps, it stopped for 5 hours during the night to give the Duce an opportunity for a short rest.

MUSSOLINI REVIEWS AN ITALIAN GUARD OF HONOUR
PRIOR TO HIS DEPARTURE FROM ROME.

3. Laura Fermi, *Mussolini* (Chicago: University of Chicago Press, 1961), p. 350.

SEPT. 25

 The following morning, the train entered Austria. There, Chancellor Dr. Kurt von Schuschnigg's cabinet was deeply concerned at the possibility of the Duce's assassination. This trip not only exposed him to the usual danger of anti-Fascist attacks, but also to a bitter hatred of the Tyrolese as a result of Italy's annexation of South Tyrol.[4] Some 4,300 Austrian soldiers were stationed along the one hundred miles of railroad line, their backs to the "Mussolini Special" with orders to "shoot to kill without question anyone suspected of bombing, shooting at or stoning the train." When Mussolini arrived at Innsbruck, he was greeted by local authorities and there he inspected the Austrian guard of honour. A short time later, as the train pulled out of Innsbruck, the Duce openly admired the scenic beauties of the little country he had championed in 1934.[5]

At 8:52 in the morning, Mussolini's train stopped at the German border town of Kiefersfelden. There, Reichsminister Hess and the Italian Ambassador Attolico met the Duce and boarded his special car. After a brief ride, the armoured train entered the lush Bavarian meadowlands and at 10 a.m. arrived at Munich.[6] As the train slowly entered the outskirts, the city seemed aflame with masses of red, white and black swastika flags fluttering beside the warmer Italian combination of red, white and green. A smile lighted Mussolini's face

4. The southern Tyrol was taken from Austria and awarded to Italy at Versailles. William L. Shirer, *The Rise and Fall of the Third Reich* (New York: Simon and Schuster, 1960), p. 337fn.

5. Details of the Hitler/Mussolini split in 1934 are discussed in Ivone Kirkpatrick's *Mussolini—A Study in Power* (New York: Hawthorn Books, Inc., 1964), pp. 294-298.

6. The trip from the Austrian border to Munich was lined with BDM members (girls from fourteen to twenty) and Jungvolk (boys from ten to fourteen) who mustered on the platforms of every station to wave welcome. *London Times*, September 25, 1937.

THE DUCE REVIEWS THE AUSTRIAN GUARD OF HONOUR AT INNSBRUCK.

MUSSOLINI VIEWS THE SCENIC AUSTRIAN COUNTRYSIDE
AS HE APPROACHES THE GERMAN BORDER.

"GERMANY WELCOMES THE DUCE," READS THE SIGN
ABOVE THE KIEFERSFELDEN RAILROAD STATION.

13

ULRICH VON HASSELL, GENERAL LIST, RUDOLF HESS, ITALIAN AMBASSADOR ATTOLICO AND HANS FRANK AWAIT THE ARRIVAL OF MUSSOLINI AT THE GERMAN BORDER TOWN OF KIEFERSFELDEN.

as the train eased into the Central Station. Everywhere, he saw tall pillars surmounted by Roman eagles and spectacular scarlet and gold caesarean festoons set off by Nordic fir and laurel. When the train halted, he was the first to step off. Adolf Hitler and his group of diplomats[7] exchanged the Fascist salute with their Italian guest, then shook hands smiling. Mussolini introduced the members of his immediate retinue, then hailed those of Hitler.

7. Among Hitler's official group was Dr. Joseph Goebbels, Minister of Propaganda; Heinrich Himmler, head of the German Police and commander of the SS; Dr. Alfred Rosenberg, in charge of Party ideological schooling; Baldur von Schirach, Reich Youth leader; Col. Gen. Werner von Fritsch, Chief of Staff; Dr. Robert Ley, leader of the German Labor Front; Viktor Lutze, commander of the SA; General Franz Ritter von Epp, Governor of Bavaria; Adolf Wagner, Bavarian Nazi leader; Ernst Wilhelm Bohle, leader of Germans living abroad; Konstantin Hierl, Labor Corps leader; and a number of less known dignitaries. *New York Times*, September 25, 1937, p. 9.

THE DUCE ARRIVES IN MUNICH.

The Duce and the Führer marched, side by side, through the station on a crimson carpet and emerged to the roar of heavy German guns crashing twenty-one times in salute. As they came in sight of the decorated Bahnhofplatz, a wide square in front of the station, they were met by the glitter of steel and standards from Army and Nazi honour detachments. Massed bands spontaneously broke into "Giovinezza," the Fascist hymn, and cheering squads set up rounds of "Heil Hitler" and "Duce, Duce!" After an inspection of the guard of honour, which was comprised of one company each from the Army, Navy, Air Force, SS, Labor Corps and the SA, the dictators entered an open Mercedes. They were slowly driven through the Munich streets where double lined SS troops stood shoulder to shoulder. Mussolini and his retinue were taken to Prince Karl Palace where they would stay while in Munich. A short time later, Hess called on the Duce and escorted him to the Führerhaus at 6 Prinzregentenstrasse. At 11:32 a.m. the two leaders met for an extended conversation in Hitler's modest five-room apartment. Count Galeazzo Ciano and Baron Constantine von Neurath, the German Foreign Minister, also participated in these talks. The discussions were general rather than particular and all that emerged was a firm agreement on a friendly attitude toward Japan and the greatest possible support to Franco in Spain. At this time, the Duce presented his host with a commission as a Corporal of Honour in the Fascist Militia, which had

THE FIRST MEETING OF THE FÜHRER
AND THE DUCE ON GERMAN SOIL.

HITLER AND MUSSOLINI MARCH THROUGH THE BAHNHOF
PAST SALUTING GERMAN DIGNITARIES.

AS THE TWO LEADERS LEAVE THE BAHNHOF,
MASSED BANDS BREAK INTO "GIOVINEZZA."

17

originally been created for himself alone.[8] In turn, the Führer bestowed upon the Duce one of Germany's highest awards, the Eagle Order, Grand Cross in gold and diamonds, which was not to be repeated for any future holder.

8. The citation awarded with the Corporal of Honour commission was signed by the Duce, and stated, "As leader of the German people, he (Hitler) has given Germany faith to new greatness. As restorer of civil, social and political order in Germany he is guiding the German nation with a firm hand to its high destiny. As representative and protector of European civilization against any attempt to destroy it, he has proven his unconditional solidarity and friendship with Italy in the hour of struggle." *Keesing's Contemporary Archives, 1937-1940*, Vol. III, (London: Keesing's Publications Limited), p. 2754.

HITLER AND MUSSOLINI REVIEW THE ARMY GUARD OF HONOUR ON THE BAHNHOFPLATZ.

INSPECTION OF THE AIR FORCE GUARD OF HONOUR.

MUSSOLINI APPROACHES THE COMMANDER
OF THE SS GUARD OF HONOUR.

REVIEW OF THE LABOR CORPS GUARD OF HONOUR.

A THIRTY-FOOT HIGH ARCH DRAPED IN FASCIST BLACK AND
WREATHED WITH LAUREL WAS ERECTED AT THE ENTRANCE
TO KARLSPLATZ, NEAR THE CITY HALL. AT ITS APEX WAS A
HUGE GILTED "M" AND ON ITS SIDES, GOLDEN FASCES.

A BEDECKED MUNICH
WELCOMES THE DUCE.

24

MUSSOLINI IS VISIBLY
IMPRESSED BY HIS WELCOME
IN MUNICH.

THE MOTORCADE MOVES DOWN LUDWIGSTRASSE TOWARD THE VICTORY STATUE.

MUSSOLINI AND HITLER.

ALFIERI AND DR. GOEBBELS.

VON NEURATH AND COUNT CIANO.

WHILE IN MUNICH, MUSSOLINI STAYS
AT THE PRINCE KARL PALACE.

REICHSMINISTER HESS CALLS ON MUSSOLINI
AND ESCORTS HIM TO THE FÜHRERHAUS.

HITLER'S CORPORAL OF HONOUR
CHEVRON WITH FASCES.

Presidenza del Consiglio dei Ministri

Comando Generale della M. V. S. N.

Adolfo Hitler

Führer e Cancelliere del Reich

è nominato

Caporale d'Onore della M. V. S. N.

« *Condottiero del Popolo Tedesco, ha dato alla Germania la fede nella sua nuova grandezza. Ricostruttore dell'ordine civile, sociale e politico tedesco guida, con fermissima mano, la Nazione Germanica verso i suoi alti destini.*

Assertore e difensore della civiltà europea contro ogni tentativo di sovvertimento, ha dato all'Italia, in ore di lotta, la sua più leale solidarietà ed amicizia ».

Dato a Roma li 24 Settembre 1937 XV E. F.

Il Comandante Generale

Mussolini

"CORPORAL OF HONOUR" CITATION AWARDED TO HITLER (SEE FOOTNOTE 8 ON PAGE 18 FOR ENGLISH TRANSLATION).

30

MUSSOLINI'S SPECIAL
EAGLE ORDER WITH GRAND
CROSS IN GOLD AND
DIAMONDS.

31

The early part of the afternoon was spent touring the carnival-decked streets and palaces and laying wreaths on various Nazi monuments in the Bavarian capital. Among these was the Feldherrnhalle in Königsplatz which held the bodies of sixteen Nazi heroes killed in the 1923 Munich Putsch. The two leaders later attended a lunch at the Führerhaus with members of the Alte Kämpfer (old fighters) of the Party. A massive parade was next on the agenda which featured Party formations. The Königsplatz resounded to the stomp of boots as Mussolini looked on in admiration from his saluting base. He later commented to Hitler, "It was wonderful!" as they stood side by side on the small reviewing stand in front of the Temples of Honour. ". . . It couldn't have been better in Italy."[9] This massive demonstration left an indelible impression on the Duce.

An afternoon reception was held in their honour at the Museum of German Art. Fräulein Leni Riefenstahl, feminine arbiter of the Nazi film world, gathered more than 100 of Germany's most beautiful stage and cinema actresses for this occasion. Hitler proudly toured Mussolini through the new museum, pointing out favorite specimens and explaining at length his elaborate plans for beautifying Berlin, Munich and other cities. After the tour, the two dictators attended a tea in the Museum's restaurant. It is interesting to note, however, that at the tea the female glances were toward boxer Max Schmeling who was also a guest. At this time, Mussolini spoke of an impending visit to Rome by Hitler. "It will be an occasion for wearing my new uniform," replied Hitler, commenting on his newly acquired rank of Corporal of Honour.[10]

That evening, Hitler and Mussolini boarded separate trains, lest perchance one wreck kill them both, which sped across Germany to the Baltic province of Mecklenburg-Schwerin.

MUSSOLINI AND HITLER REVIEW THE "LEIBSTANDARTE ADOLF HITLER" ON THEIR WAY TO THE FELDHERRNHALLE.

---

9. *New York Times*, September 26, 1937, p. 1.
10. *Time*, October 4, 1937, p. 20.

NOTE THE CUFF TITLE ON THE UNIFORMS OF
"LEIBSTANDARTE ADOLF HITLER" MEMBERS AT LEFT.

SILVER EMBROIDERED "LAH" CUFF TITLE (OFFICERS).

(ABOVE) AFTER HONOURING THE FALLEN FIGHTERS OF NOVEMBER 9, 1923, MUSSOLINI AND HITLER DEPART.

(LEFT) WREATH LAYING AT THE FELDHERRNHALLE HONOUR TEMPLE, ON THE KÖNIGSPLATZ.

37

MUSSOLINI AND HITLER ARE GREETED BY THE LEADING MEN OF THE PARTY
AS THEY WALK THROUGH THE HALLS OF THE FÜHRERHAUS IN MUNICH.

AN INFORMAL CONVERSATION DURING LUNCH IN THE GREAT HALL OF THE FÜHRERHAUS.

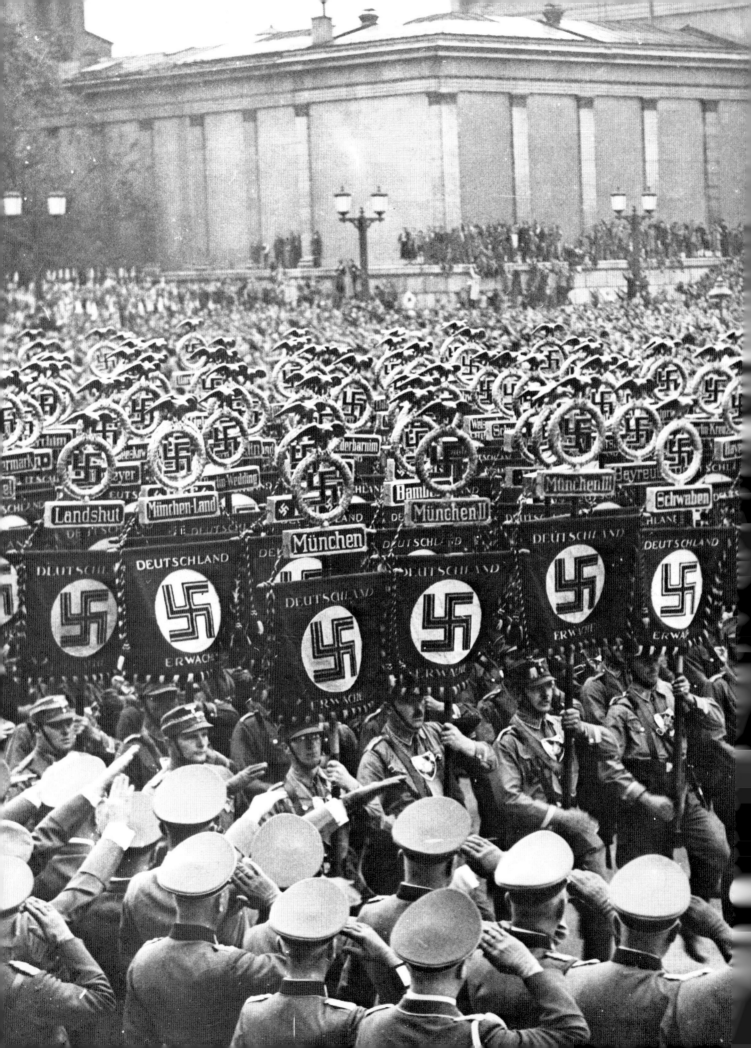

München

DEUTSCHLAND

ERWACHE

STURM-ABTEILUNG (SA)　　STANDARD FROM MUNICH.

(LEFT) MASSED SA STANDARDS PASS IN REVIEW
DURING THE GREAT PARADE ON KÖNIGSPLATZ.

41

THE SA PASSES IN REVIEW....

THE HITLER YOUTH (DEUTSCHES JUNGVOLK)....

THE SA "FELDHERRNHALLE"....

SA GRUPPE HOCHLAND" (NOTE EDELWEISS ON CAP)....

THE OLD FIGHTERS (ALTE KÄMPFER)....

THE LABOR CORPS (ARBEITSDIENST)....

A NUMBER OF GERMAN AND ITALIAN
DIGNITARIES OBSERVE THE PARADE.

THE "SS-LEIBSTANDARTE ADOLF HITLER." . . .

OFFICER'S TOTENKOPF
COLLAR PATCH.

DEATH'S HEAD (TOTENKOPF)
BATTALION FROM MUNICH.

MUSSOLINI, HITLER, COUNT CIANO, STARACE, VON HASSELL, ALFIERI AND FRANK.

THE PRIDE OF MUNICH WAS THE NEWLY CONSTRUCTED HOUSE OF GERMAN ART.

REVIEWING THE ART EXHIBITIONS.

SEPT. 26

 On the morning of September 26, they arrived at the little village of Lalendorf, near the centre of the maneuver area, to witness the final stages of post World War I Germany's greatest military maneuvers. Hitler and the Italian party were met at the station by high officials of the German defense forces which were led by War Minister Werner von Blomberg, Air Minister Hermann Göring, the Army Chief of Staff, Col. General Werner von Fritsch, and Naval Chief of Staff, Admiral Erich Raeder. In an open touring car, Hitler and Mussolini dashed from area to area observing the latest in artillery, infantry and armoured techniques. Throughout the lightning tour, they were cheered by German soldiers who were of the class of 1935. These troops had been the first to be called up when Hitler restored conscription to the German way of life.

At the conclusion of the maneuvers, Hitler and Mussolini boarded a special train to Kröpelin, in the northwestern corner of Mecklenburg-Schwerin. There, they inspected the new flying field at Wustrow, examined several new types of military aircraft and later observed air exercises.[11] Once again the Duce was visibly impressed. Up until now, Mussolini had seen German art, layed wreaths on monuments, inspected honour guards and observed war games. He now wanted to inspect one of Germany's most closely guarded secrets . . . the mighty Krupp munitions works at Essen. The German schedule had called for a short trip to Berlin from the Baltic for a triumphant welcome but Mussolini's insistence now called for the dictators to travel across Germany to Essen and then cross it once more, back to Berlin. Immediately, German Minister of Propaganda and Public Enlightenment, Dr. Paul Josef Goebbels broadcast to the astonished citizens of Essen that they were to deck their city with green branches and flags in honour of the Italian leader who would arrive the next day. To insure that all arrangements would be in readiness, Dr. Goebbels and several assistants rushed by special train to Essen.

---

11. The famous slow-flying "Storch" was demonstrated at this air exercise. Major-General Udet, with Air-General Milch as passenger, flew this versatile aircraft of minimal speeds of 12-15 m.p.h. *London Times*, September 27, 1937.

MUSSOLINI IS GREETED BY ADMIRAL RAEDER. . . .

AIR MINISTER GÖRING. . .

. . . AND DEFENSE MINISTER VON BLOMBERG.

53

AFTER THE OFFICIAL GREETINGS, THE DIPLOMATIC ENTOURAGE
IS ESCORTED TO WAITING CARS. (FROM LEFT TO RIGHT) HITLER,
COUNT CIANO, VON NEURATH, MUSSOLINI, VON BLOMBERG AND GÖRING.

THE PERSONAL STANDARDS OF
MUSSOLINI AND HITLER.

MUSSOLINI, HITLER, COLONEL SCHMUNDT (HITLER'S MILITARY ADJUTANT) AND ERICH KEMPKA (HITLER'S DRIVER) EN ROUTE TO THE MANEUVER AREA.

REVIEW OF MANEUVER ACTION.

HESS, HITLER, MUSSOLINI AND GENERAL LIST.

THE STANDARDS OF THE FÜHRER AND
THE DUCE WERE CONSTANTLY IN THEIR
PRESENCE DURING THE MANEUVERS.

(FRONT ROW) HESS, COUNT CIANO, HITLER,
UNIDENTIFIED, MUSSOLINI AND GENERAL LIST.

COUNT CIANO, FRANK AND HITLER.

MUSSOLINI, GÖRING, FRANK AND BADOGLIO.

NOTE MANEUVER MARKINGS
ON THE PZ. KPFW. I

LIGHT 37MM FLAK.

62

THE FLAK "88" IN ACTION.

63

THE AIR SHOW AT WUSTROW.

THE FIESELER "STORCH".

TAIL OF A HEINKEL HE-111.

HITLER'S STANDARD.

SEPT. 27

 After traveling across Germany in separate trains, the Hitler and Mussolini specials rumbled into Essen at 8:07 a.m. on September 27. Essen and Krupp had done themselves proud . . . all was in readiness. Due to security precautions, correspondents were not allowed to join in the tour while the Duce and the Führer inspected the hush-hush realm of munitioneer Dr. Gustav Krupp von Bohlen und Halbach. At the company's offices, the dictators were received by the director of Krupp who presented the members of his family. He then explained the growth and organization of his gigantic concern. The party was then escorted to the main plant by auto. There, they saw the production of artillery, tanks and every conceivable weapon of war. Mussolini was highly impressed by the discipline of the workers, scale of operation and the tremendous output of weaponry. The Krupp inspection ended at 10:45 a.m.

THE DUCE ARRIVES IN ESSEN.

THE DUCE REVIEWS AN SS HONOUR COMPANY
OUTSIDE THE RAILROAD STATION IN ESSEN.

"HEARTY WELCOME TO THE WEAPONS FORGE OF THE REICH."

THE STREETS OF ESSEN ARE PACKED WITH CROWDS ANTICIPATING
THE ARRIVAL OF THE OFFICIAL MOTORCADE.

DRIVING THROUGH THE STREETS OF ESSEN.

AT THE OFFICE OF KRUPP VON BOHLEN UND HALBACH.

THE JOURNEY FROM ESSEN TO BERLIN IS A JOYFUL ONE FOR THE DUCE

CHEERING CROWDS GREETED HIM AT ALL STATIONS.

Once again, the leaders traveled in separate trains from Essen. Elaborate measures were taken with true German thoroughness to ensure that for the last 15 miles of the journey to Berlin, the two trains would run side by side—signifying the parallelism of the two revolutions. Before arriving at the station, Hitler sped ahead—enabling him to be on the platform to properly greet his guest. The arrival in the German capital was, as Count Ciano stated in his diary, "Triumphal."[12]

The first three days of the state visit had been for indoctrination but the culmination was the welcoming in Berlin. Never before in German history had Berlin witnessed such a display. This spectacle dwarfed

HITLER WELCOMES HIS GUEST TO BERLIN.

12. Count Galeazzo Ciano, *Ciano's Hidden Diary, 1937-1938* (New York: E. P. Dutton and Co. Inc., 1953), p. 16.

the Munich pageantry to the dimensions of a county fair. With the aid of professional stage designer Benno von Arendt, Berlin's central sections were transformed into a prop fairyland.

The city was decorated with thousands of German and Italian flags, from the station at the Heerstrasse to the Presidential Palace in the centre of the city. A 126 foot flag tower erected in Adolf Hitler Platz, midway between the railway station and Brandenburg Gate, was bedecked with German and Italian flags thirty yards long. The Pariserplatz, before Brandenburg Gate, had two coloured water fountains and four massive towers covered alternately with Italian and German flags.[13]

IN THE HEERSTRASSE RAILROAD STATION, MUSSOLINI IS CORDIALLY WELCOMED BY LEADING MEN OF THE REICH.

13. *New York Times*, September 27, 1937, p. 8.

Dusk fell as the leaders drove through the floodlit Brandenburg Gate onto the famous Unter den Linden. There, four rows of white illuminated pylons, thirty-three feet high, bearing golden eagles and Nazi and Fascist emblems, glowed in the night. Banners in the German and Italian colours hung from roofs to sidewalks in this street and in the Wilhelmstrasse. It is estimated that approximately 55,000 square yards of bunting had been woven for the decoration of these two streets. As the crowds roared a welcome to the Italian dictator, Mussolini stood up to let himself be seen, obviously delighted with his reception. The Führer remained seated at his left, allowing his guest to enjoy the full glory of the moment.

Work had ceased in Berlin at 4 p.m. on the day of the arrival, enabling the total population to be present. The next day was declared

a public holiday. Hitler took personal precautions in the security measures asserted to protect the Duce. Approximately 60,000 SS troops lined the route of travel. In some places they stood three and four deep. The city's police was reinforced by detachments from Saxony. Plainclothesmen mixed in the crowd while armed launches patrolled the Spree River.

That evening a state banquet was held in Mussolini's honour. Members of government and all leading members of the Party were present at the Berlin reception. Hitler, a strict vegetarian and teetotaler, nibbled throughout the banquet and toasted his guest with sweet German champagne. The menu of the evening consisted of sole, chicken, caviar, soup, ices and fresh fruit.[14]

PASSING THROUGH THE BRANDENBURG GATE
AND ENTERING UNTER DEN LINDEN.

14. *Time*, October 11, 1937, p. 23.

PHILIPP BOUHLER, ACHILLE STARACE, AND
DR. ROBERT LEY WITH TWO FASCIST OFFICIALS.

A FASCIST MILITIA COLONEL AND A FASCIST
SERGEANT AT THE STATE BANQUET IN BERLIN.

WALTER FUNK AND DINO ALFIERI WITH THREE
FASCIST MILITIA OFFICIALS.

(ABOVE) BELLEVUE CASTLE—CONSTRUCTED IN 1785 BY M. PH. BOUMANN FOR FERDINAND, THE YOUNGEST BROTHER OF FREDERICK THE GREAT. (BELOW) NORTH FACADE OF THE BERLIN PALACE.

Central Berlin

PARISER-
PLATZ

UNTER DEN LINDEN

CHARLOTTENBURGER
CHAUSSEE

1. ITALIAN EMBASSY
2. REICHSTAG
3. BRANDENBURG GATE
4. REICHSCHANCELLERY
5. FREDERICK THE GREAT STATUE
6. UNIVERSITY
7. EHRENMAL (WAR MEMORIAL)
8. ZEUGHAUS (ARMORY)
9. LUSTGARTEN
10. BERLIN PALACE

(RIGHT) UNTER DEN LINDEN AS SEEN FROM
THE BRANDENBURG GATE, LOOKING EAST.

THE DUCE RESIDED IN THE
HISTORICAL PALACE OF THE REICHS-
PRESIDENT WHILE VISITING BERLIN.
NOTE MUSSOLINI'S PERSONAL
STANDARD ON THE FLAGPOLE ATOP
THE BUILDING.

AN ARMY GUARD AT THE MAIN ENTRANCE
E PALACE OF THE REICHSPRESIDENT.

Unter den Linden

BERLINERS CROWD ONTO UNTER DEN LINDEN FOR A MOMENT'S GLANCE AT HITLER AND MUSSOLINI. NOTE THE NEWLY PLANTED LINDEN TREES WHICH ADORN BOTH SIDES OF THIS AVENUE. THEY REPLACED THE OLD LINDEN TREES WHICH WERE DESTROYED DURING SUBWAY CONSTRUCTION THE PREVIOUS YEAR.

MUSSOLINI AND HITLER ARE DRIVEN DOWN
THE CHARLOTTENBURGER CHAUSSEE.

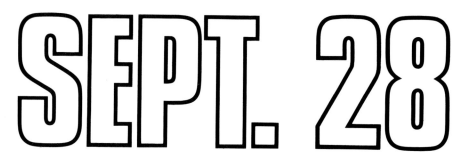

SEPT. 28

 The following morning, Mussolini visited the Arsenal Museum on Unter den Linden where he viewed mementoes from previous wars. He also stood reverently, for a few minutes, before President von Hindenburg's death mask. He and his party then motored to Potsdam, near Berlin, and inspected Sanssouci, Frederick the Great's palace. After walking to the famous Garrison Church, Mussolini placed a wreath on the tomb of Frederick the Great. The Duce then returned to Berlin and called on the Italian Embassy and the headquarters of Fascio. There he was saluted by 25,000 Italian Fascists now resident in Germany and 3,500 members of the Fascist youth organization.

At noon he drove with Ciano and Bernardo Attolico, his new Ambassador to Berlin, to Schorfheide, forty miles from Berlin. He then attended a luncheon given by Göring and his wife at their beautiful hunting lodge, Waldhof Karinhall. It was at this time that he was presented with the Luftwaffe's highest award—the Pilot-Observer badge in gold with diamonds. Later, he took afternoon tea with Dr. Goebbels and then retired to the Presidential Palace where he dined privately that evening.

Simultaneously that day, a mammoth demonstration was being organized on the Maifeld, the polo ground adjoining the Olympic Stadium. Since early that morning a crowd of approximately 650,000 had gone to the city's outskirts and gathered before the official tribune. At 6 p.m. the Olympic Bell began to ring, signifying that Hitler and Mussolini were en route. Their arrival was announced by trumpets while the large personal standards of the Duce and the Führer were hoisted on either side of the tribune.

Despite threatening rain clouds, the crowd was good-natured. Before the speakers ascended the tribune, the crowd amused itself by protesting the huge floodlights which dazzled many eyes. "Hermann, verdunkeln!"—that is, "Hermann, make it dark!"—the crowd chorused to General Göring, with memories of the recent Berlin blackout exercise. In response, Göring came forward and saluted, but the lights were not dimmed.[15]

15. *New York Times*, September 29, 1937, p. 12.

THE DUCE'S AUTOGRAPH IS GIVEN TO A POTSDAM YOUTH.

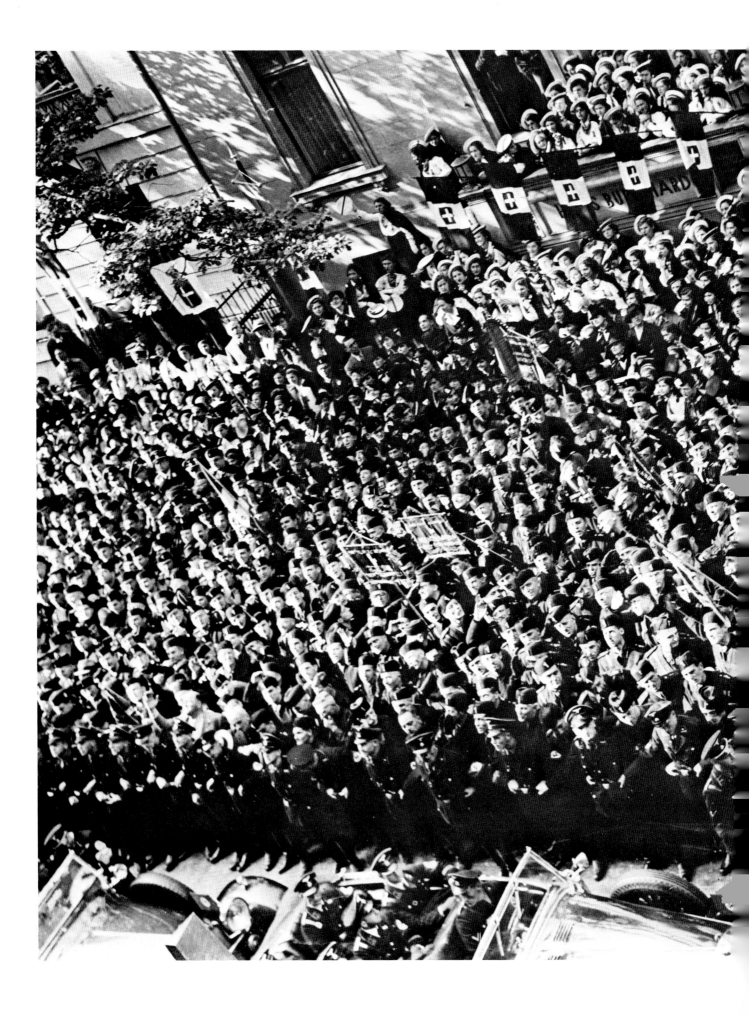

(ABOVE) THE MUSSOLINI MOTORCADE ARRIVES AT THE HEADQUARTERS OF FASCIO.

(BELOW) MUSSOLINI SIGNS THE OFFICIAL GUEST BOOK.

ITALIAN DIPLOMATIC AND
FASCIST LEADERS AWAIT-
ING THE ARRIVAL OF THE
DUCE AT THE ITALIAN
EMBASSY.

(RIGHT) THE DUCE IS VISIBLY MOV
THE CHEERING FASCIST CROWDS B

MUSSOLINI ACCOMPANIED BY ITALIAN AMBASSADOR ATTOLICO
VISITS HIS BERLIN STAFF AND THEIR WIVES.

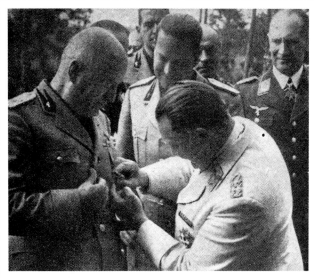

THE AIR FORCE'S HIGHEST AWARD
IS BESTOWED UPON THE DUCE.

AFTER PRESENTATION OF THE GOLDEN
PILOT-OBSERVER BADGE, MUSSOLINI
CONVERSES WITH GÖRING AND AIR FORCE
GENERAL LÖRZER.

PILOT-OBSERVER BADGE IN GOLD WITH DIAMONDS.

THE OFFICIAL MOTORCADE EN ROUTE TO THE MAIFELD.

THE MAIFELD . . . WHERE HITLER AND MUSSOLINI DELIVER THEIR SPEECHES HEARD ROUND-THE-WORLD.

(RIGHT) A VIEW OF THE OL
STADIUM FROM THE MAIFE

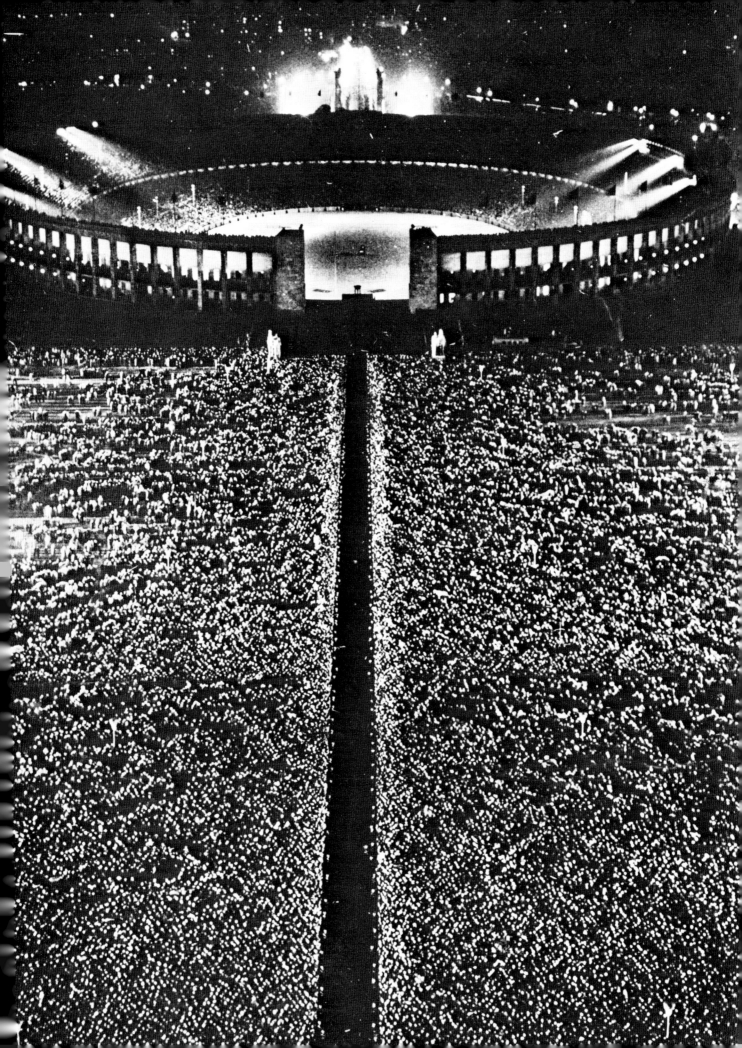

DR. GOEBBELS INTRODUCES THE FÜHRER AND THE DUCE.

Dr. Goebbels mounted the speaker's tribune and stated, "Three million people have taken part in this historic demonstration of the National Socialist movement, either along the route, on the Maifeld or in the Stadium." All of Germany's radio stations were connected to the Maifeld speaker system. Twenty countries, in Europe and North and South America, were also united in the gigantic hook-up which the Propaganda Ministry had arranged for this occasion. Great Britain did not accept the broadcast, however, and Russia was not invited to do so. As Dr. Goebbels, the man who had supervised this engineering wonder, told the two dictators in presenting them to the audience— "The whole world is listening to you!"[16]

Hitler was the first to speak to the German nation by wireless. He introduced the Duce: "What moves us most at the moment is the deep-rooted joy to see in our midst a guest who is one of the lonely men in history who are not put to trial by historic events but determine the history of their country themselves." Mussolini then stood up and climbed the podium to speak. Before him, thousands of German arms rose in the Roman salute. Mussolini delivered his carefully prepared speech in fluent German, but with an Italian accent. In the midst of Duce's speech, a darkening sky suddenly opened and a torrential rain fell on the Maifeld. Unfortunately he became overcome by the excitement generated by the dynamic spectacle before him and spoke faster and faster. This, plus the sounds of the downpour caused his words to be almost inaudible. His script was soon a sodden mass but he continued as the patient crowd became soaked to the skin. In the course of his speech the Duce pronounced, "Fascism has its ethical principles, to which it intends to be faithful, and they are also my morals; to speak clearly and openly, and, if we are friends, to march together to the end." He also spoke of the awakening of Germany through the Nazi revolution, Bolshevism—the common enemy— and Germany's friendly stand during the Ethiopian War. The speech ended with a stress on the 115 million Germans and Italians and the need for them to unite "in one single, unshakable determination."

After the speeches, Hitler and Mussolini walked across the field to the Olympic Stadium. There, in the huge green and brown Olympic arena, marched the massed bands of three Army corps. There were 4,000 musicians in all . . . 33 brass bands, 25 fife and drum corps and 10 trumpet bands. They goosestepped in perfect precision to the tune of "Preussens Gloria," a favorite military march, and wheeled into three columns in the centre of the arena. The trumpet bands came from the cavalry and artillery and the rest of the units from the Army, Navy and Air Force. As the floodlights shone on them, the

16. *Ibid.*

massed musicians sent forth strains of the great marches from Verdi's "Aida," for the Italians' benefit, and Wagner's "Rienzi," for the Germans. Then the "Bavarian March Past" was struck up and from under an arch, at the side of the Stadium, a battalion of torchbearing Schutzstaffeln (Hitler's elite SS guards) appeared. They flowed into the arena like a living flame, wheeling halfway around, dividing and moving to each side in columns of four. These again divided and became streamlets of two's, which in turn divided, countermarched and passed each other in single file just as a second torchbearing battalion came from under the arch. The first battalion marched in single file around the arena and took rigid stations at its edges, approximately three yards apart. The second battalion divided, subdivided and moved through the massed musicians, forming with them a huge "M" with its base toward the dais on which Hitler and Mussolini stood. After this complicated maneuver, the musicians began a march by Beethoven. Simultaneously, three "honour companies" from the Army, Navy and Air Force entered. They goosestepped halfway around the arena, then wheeled to the front and came to attention. Their mounted commander came forward, faced the dais, and reported to Hitler, "1,600 of your defense forces, mein Führer."

Outside the stadium, 50 concealed searchlights threw up long beams of light, forming "the tent of light" which was now a feature at German pageants. The troops came to present arms and the massed bands very softly played the German Army hymn, followed by the Italian national anthem, "Giovinezza," "Deutschland über Alles" and the "Horst Wessel Lied."[17]

As the spectacle came to an end, the rain began to fall once more. Standing equally unprotected, side by side, Mussolini made a remark to Hitler. Hitler made a gesture to a nearby SS officer who threw rain capes around the shoulders of both leaders. The end of this massive pageant came when the huge swastika and Fascist standards, above the host and guest, were lowered as they departed from the Stadium.[18]

---

17. *New York Times*, September 29, 1937, p. 12.
18. Ciano's comments of this event were ". . . choreography superb—much emotion and much rain." Ciano, *Ciano's Hidden Diary*, p. 16.

Text of the Hitler Speech

We have just witnessed a historic event, the significance of which has no parallel. More than a million people have gathered here, participating in a demonstration which is being closely followed by the national communities of two countries, numbering one hundred and fifteen millions, besides hundreds of millions more in other parts of the world who were following the proceedings over the radio as more or less interested listeners.

What moves us the most at this moment is the deep-rooted joy to see in our midst a guest who is one of the lonely men in history who are not put to trial by historic events but determine the history of their country themselves.

Secondly, we realize that this demonstration is not one of those meetings which we can experience anywhere. It is an avowal of common ideals and common interests. It is the avowal pronounced by two men and it is heard by a million people assembled before us, an avowal which is expected by and is the concern of one hundred and fifteen millions with a burning heart.

That is why the present demonstration is more than a public meeting. It is a manifestation of nations. The true meaning of this public gathering consists of the sincere desire to guarantee a peace to our two countries which is not the reward for resigned cowardice but the result of a responsible policy safeguarding the racial intellect and physical fitness of the nation as well as its cultural possessions. In doing this we hope to serve the interests of two nations and, more than that, the interests of the European Continent.

The fact that we are in a position today to hold this meeting reminds us of the changes that have taken place in the period which we have left behind us. There is no nation in the world which longs more for peace than Germany and no country has suffered more from the terrible consequences of misplaced blind confidence than our nation. We recall a period of fifteen years before National Socialism came into power, a time which was marked by oppression, exploitation, the denial of equal rights with other nations and with unutterable mental torture and material distress.

The ideals of liberalism and democracy have not preserved the German nation from the worst depression history has ever seen. National Socialism was thus forced to create a new ideal and a more effective one, according all human rights to our people which had been denied the nation for fifteen long years.

During this time of bitter experience Italy, and Fascist Italy especially, refused to take part in the humiliation Germany was subjected to. I must make it a point to say

this tonight before the German people and the whole world. In the course of these years, Italy has shown understanding for the demands of a great nation claiming equal rights with other peoples in the endeavor to provide the means of subsistence and, above all, to save its honor.

We are only too glad that the hour has come in which we are given the opportunity to recall the past and, I believe, we have remembered our debt of gratitude.

The common trend of ideas expressed in the Fascist and National Socialist revolutions has developed today into a similar course of action. This will have a salutary influence on the world, in which destruction and deformation are trying to win the upper hand. Fascist Italy has been transformed into a new imperial Romanum by the ingenious activities of a compelling personality.

You, Benito Mussolini, will have realized that in these days, due to the National Socialist State, Germany has become a great power, thanks to her racial attitude and her military strength. The inherent strength of the two countries is the best guarantee for the preservation of Europe, which is inspired by a sense of responsibility in the discharge of its cultural mission. It is not willing to allow destructive elements to cause its decline and dissolution.

You who are present at this very hour and those who are listening to us in other parts of the world must acknowledge that two sovereign national regimes have come into contact at a time in which the democratic and Marxist International revels in demonstrations of hatred which must result in dissension. Every attempt to interfere with the understanding between the two nations or to play one up against the other by casting suspicion and by obscuring the real aims in order to dissolve the ideal partnership will be of no avail because of the innermost desire of one hundred and fifteen million people, who are united at the manifestation of this very hour, and because of the determination of the two men who are standing here to address you.

Text of the Mussolini Speech

Comrades, my visit to this country must not be judged by the standards of an ordinary diplomatic political visit. The fact that I have come to Germany today does not imply that I shall travel to some other city tomorrow. I have not come here in the capacity of chief of the Italian Government. I am standing here as the leader of a national revolution giving proof of the strong ties uniting me with your revolutionary movement. There are no ulterior motives connected with my journey and no secret intentions. There will be no scheme here which would tend to menace divided Europe still further. The confirmation of the unshaken axis Rome-Berlin is not directed against other states.

In answer to the question posed by the whole world, "What will be the outcome of the meeting in Berlin, war or peace?" we — the Führer and myself — reply in a loud voice, "Peace."

If people will take the trouble to study the national revolutions in Germany and in Italy there will be far less prejudice, and many points for argument will soon be eliminated. We share many of the fundamental principles in our respective ideologies. National socialism and fascism do not only have the same enemies in the world who serve the same master, the Third International, but they share an elevated conception of life and history.

Germany and Italy likewise pursue the same policy in the economic sphere, a policy of economic autarchy, for the political freedom of a nation can only be guaranteed by its economic independence. A nation, strong from the military point of view, might easily become the victim of an economic blockade. We Italians were threatened by that great danger last year when fifty-two nations at Geneva decided to impose economic sanctions against us which, although they finally failed, were nevertheless a great threat to our very existence, and in the end only showed the world what Fascist Italy was able to achieve.

We shall never forget that Germany was not among the nations which imposed sanctions against us. That was the time when the first signs of the necessity for cooperation between Fascist Italy and National Socialist Germany appeared on the political horizon. What is nowadays known by the term "axis Rome-Berlin" actually came into existence in Autumn, 1935, and ever since then the Italy-Germany solidarity has been constantly strengthened and it has done everything to promote peace in Europe.

Fascism has its own ethics and we intend to adhere thereto in any circumstance, and these ethics of ours oblige us always to be frank and outspoken with everybody, and once we have made real friends with any one, to remain faithful to him to the last. All arguments which

our opponents employ against us are of no avail, because there exists no dictatorship, neither in Germany nor in Italy, but there exist organizations which really serve the good of the peoples.

No government in the whole world enjoys the confidence of their peoples as much as do the Italian and German Governments. The greatest and soundest democracies which exist in the world today are Italy and Germany. Elsewhere, politics are dominated by the great powers of capitalism, by secret societies and political groups which work against each other under the pretext of the so-called "inalienable rights of humanity."

In Germany and Italy it is absolutely impossible that politics be interfered with or influenced by private persons. Everything that Germany and Italy have in common is most clearly expressed in their joint struggle against bolshevism, which is the modern counterpart of the darkest Byzantine tyranny — that unparalleled exploitation of the trustfulness of lower races, that regime of starvation, bloodshed and slavery.

Since the war fascism has fought against this scourge of humanity and the depression which it has nourished, and fought against it with all its might by word and deed. Thus did we fight in Spain, where thousands of Italian Fascist volunteers have fallen for the sake of Europe's culture, a culture which may yet see a revival if it will but turn a deaf ear on the false prophets in Geneva and Moscow and turn to the burning realities of our revolutions.

Comrades, beyond the frontiers of our own country we, like you, make no propaganda in the ordinary sense of the word in order to gain adherents. We believe that truth by itself is powerful enough to penetrate all barriers and that truth will finally conquer. The Europe of tomorrow will be Fascist by the logical sequence of events but not by our propaganda.

It is nearly twenty years ago since your great leader sent forth to the masses his appeal for a revolution — that appeal, which was destined to become the battlecry of the entire German nation, "Deutschland Erwache." Germany has roused herself. The Third Reich is an accomplished fact. I do not know whether and when Europe will awake, for secret forces not unknown to us are at work striving to transform a civil war into a world conflagration.

It is of the utmost importance that our two peoples, which together count no less than one hundred and fifteen million souls, stand firm and united with the same unswerving confidence. Today's tremendous demonstration has given the world proof of this.

AN ARMY TRUMPET BAND SENDING
FORTH STRAINS OF "PREUSSENS GLORIA."

AT THE CONCLUSION OF THE STADIUM FESTIVITIES,
THE RAIN BEGAN TO FALL ONCE MORE.

PORTIONS OF THE MASSED BANDS IN THE OLYMPIC STADIUM.

THE CURTAIN CLOSES A FESTIVE AND WET SPECTACLE.

109

SEPT. 29

The morning activities were confined to the placing of a magnificent wreath at the German War Memorial on Unter den Linden by Mussolini, Count Ciano and Marshal Badoglio. The wreath's green, white and red ribbon bore the inscription "Benito Mussolini Anno XV." After reviewing the guard of honour at the War Memorial, Mussolini marched past about 100 war invalids in self-propelled wheelchairs and saluted them.

He then joined Hitler in a salute to 14,000 men of the Army, Navy and Air Force on Charlottenburger Chaussee. The parade, which was led by General Witzleben, commander of the Third Army Group, took 1 hour and 20 minutes. 591 officers, 13,000 rank and file, 2,000 horses, 600 motorized vehicles and 144 motorcycle units, all drawn from Berlin and neighboring garrisons, passed by. The Army contingent was comprised of 5 infantry regiments, 4 artillery, 1 cavalry, besides pioneer, armoured, signal and machine-gun battalions. The Air Force contributed 3 motorized A-A regiments while the Navy contributed two companies of cadets.[19]

AN ARMY HONOUR COMPANY MARCHES TO THE WAR MEMORIAL FOR THE DUCE'S INSPECTION.

19. The Duce later spoke to his wife of some amusing incidents which occurred during the parade. "During the military review the mace bearer was too quick and struck a soldier behind him on the head, and an artillery horse kicked over the traces and bolted right in front of the box. Hitler laughed and so did I. Then he turned to me and remarked confidentially, 'I don't like to think what'll happen to that wretched private. Our perfect German organization will be set in motion. The general will go for the colonel; the colonel will go for the major; the major will go for the captain; the captain will go for the lieutenant; the lieutenant will go for the sergeant-major; the sergeant-major for the sergeant; the sergeant for the corporal; and finally . . . poor private!'" Mussolini, *My Life with Mussolini*, p. 93.

MUSSOLINI REVIEWS THE HONOUR COMPANY NEAR
THE WAR MEMORIAL ON UNTER DEN LINDEN.

MUSSOLINI'S WREATH WHICH WAS LATER
PLACED AT THE WAR MEMORIAL.

WREATHS ARE LAYED IN THE WAR MEMORIAL
BY MUSSOLINI AND HIS ENTOURAGE.

MUSSOLINI AND HIS ENTOURAGE OF GERMAN AND ITALIAN DIGNITARIES EMERGE FROM THE WAR MEMORIAL (EHRENMAL).
ORIGINALLY BUILT IN 1816 BY SCHINKEL AND NAMED THE NEW GUARDHOUSE (NEUE WACHE), IT WAS CONVERTED IN
1931 TO A MEMORIAL IN HONOUR OF THE FALLEN IN WORLD WAR I.

. . . AS A PARADE OF HONOUR
COMPANIES ASSEMBLES.

STARACE, ALFIERI,
FRANK AND BADOGLIO.

ULRICH VON HASSELL, GERMAN
AMBASSADOR TO ITALY FROM
1932 to 1937 (NOTE NSKK
BRIGADEFÜHRER UNIFORM).

Al Camerata Ministro Hans Frank
con viva cordialità
Berlino 29 Sett. 1937-XV   Mussolini

AN ARMY OFFICER STEPS FORWARD AND
SIGNALS THE MARCH-BY TO BEGIN.

PORTRAIT OF THE DUCE PRESENTED TO HANS FRANK ON
MBER 29, 1937 BY MUSSOLINI (AUTHOR'S COLLECTION).

PARADE AT THE WAR MEMORIAL.

THE DUCE SALUTES GERMAN
INVALIDS FROM WORLD WAR I.

GENERAL VON BLOMBERG, MUSSOLINI AND HITLER AWAIT THE

REGIMENTAL STANDARDS.

INFANTRY UNITS

ARMY MOTORCYCLE UNITS.

AIR FORCE PERSONNEL.

COMMANDER, MOTORIZED ARTILLERY WITH STANDARD.

ARTILLERY STANDARD.

ARMOURED UNITS.

127

(ABOVE) THE PARADE PROGRESSES PAST
GENERAL VON BLOMBERG, MUSSOLINI,
HITLER, ADMIRAL RAEDER AND GENERAL
FREIHERR VON FRITSCH.

(RIGHT) GENERAL LIST, VON
HASSELL, COUNT CIANO, FRANK,
STARACE AND ALFIERI.

ARTILLERY UNITS.
ARMED ARTILLERY CREWS ON CAISSONS.

(ABOVE) A CAVALRY SQUADRON.

(BELOW) A MACHINE-GUN BATTALION.

130

GENERAL BADOGLIO CONGRATULATES HITLER UPON
COMPLETION OF HIS GRAND MILITARY REVIEW.

After the impressive review, Mussolini was taken to the Reichs Chancellery for a farewell luncheon. He was then escorted to the Lehrter
Station in Berlin. There, he and Hitler shook hands heartily and continued an animated conversation from his window, after the Duce had
boarded the train. Personal gifts accompanied him . . . three crates
of geese presented by the curator of the Berlin Zoological Gardens.
The city of Hannover gave equestrian Mussolini a silver statuette of
a charger, the original to be sent to him in Rome.[20] Hess, Hitler's
deputy, traveled with the Italian party as far as the German frontier.
German and Italian bodyguards were stationed throughout the train
and armed police guarded the railroad bridges.

After dining with Hess and von Bülow-Schwante, head of the protocol
department of the German Foreign Ministry, Mussolini privately asked
von Bülow-Schwante to express his (Mussolini's) sincerest gratitude
and his most friendly feelings to the Führer and Chancellor. He also
stated that he had come to Germany with great expectations, but what
he had experienced had exceeded these. His admiration for the
Führer, for the German people, and for their achievements was in-
finitely great. He further expressed his appreciation for the fact that
all his wishes, even regarding the character of his visit, had been
fulfilled through the arrangement of the program, as well as for the
courteous reception accorded him.[21]

20. This gift was awarded to Mussolini at a brief stop at Hanover during
the trip from Essen to Berlin. *New York Times*, September 27, 1937, p. 8.

21. *Documents on German Foreign Policy*. Memorandum from von-Bülow-
Schwante to the Foreign Minister via the State Secretary. Berlin, October 2, 1937.

BY NOON, THE BERLIN CROWDS WERE MASSING IN THE PARISERPLATZ
FOR A FINAL FAREWELL TO THE DUCE (NOTE THE DOME OF THE REICHSTAG
IN THE UPPER CENTER OF THE PHOTO).

132

GERMAN FLAG TOWER IN PARISERPLATZ. ITALIAN FLAG TOWER IN THE PARISERPLATZ.

(ABOVE) BRANDENBURG GATE.

(BELOW) CROWDS IN THE PARISERPLAT

THE CHARLOTTENBURGER CHAUSSEE SWELLS WITH BERLINERS
TRYING TO GET A FINAL GLIMPSE OF THE DUCE AND HITLER
EN ROUTE TO THE LEHRTER RAILROAD STATION.

A FRIENDLY CONVERSATION CONTINUES
FROM THE DUCE'S TRAIN WINDOW.

(RIGHT) HITLE
FAREWELL SAI

In Germany, Mussolini's success was doubtful, as most Germans were unimpressed by him and the value of the Italian alliance. The Duce, however, was intoxicated by the German spectacle of power and fascinated by Hitler, the man. Here was, indeed, an ally who would be profitable to join and dangerous to cross.

Mussolini's return to Rome was triumphal. Arches and laurel, which were the symbols of conquerors in war, greeted him everywhere. He later spoke of the new relations between Italy and Germany, with his wife Rachele, and the purposes of the Anti-Comintern Pact and the Pact of Steel. "We are trying to create a firm antibolshevik front in Europe, stretching from the North Sea to the Mediterranean. The Führer and I have sized up the Moscovite move in Spain in exactly the same way. It can be said that Spain has given us our first opportunity for a vigorous plan for common defense against bolshevism. We shall make every effort to extend and strengthen this defensive system. But defensive it is, as I see it, with no immediate military objectives and there is nothing aggressive about it. If we could build up a block of nations that really matter, I think it would be enough to induce Moscow to confine its field of activities and experiments to its own nationals."[22]

Thus Benito Mussolini fell under the influence of Adolf Hitler . . . an influence that would sometimes be strained due to the stresses of war but always revived when the two met.

---

22. Mussolini, *My Life with Mussolini*, p. 93.

(RIGHT) THE ARRIVES IN

ANS CHEER MUSSOLINI
N HIS ARRIVAL TO THE CITY.

DUCE REVIEWS AN ITALIAN
Y GUARD OF HONOUR.

HEN REVIEWS A PUBLIC
RITY POLICE UNIT.

MUSSOLINI AND COUNT CIANO PREPARE TO DRIVE THROUGH
THE STREETS OF ROME TO THE PALAZZO VENEZIA.

THOUSANDS OF ITALIANS MASS IN FRONT OF THE PALAZZO VENEZIA
TO HEAR THE DUCE'S ADDRESS CONCERNING HIS STATE VISIT.

Bibliography

Berliner Illustrirte Zeitung, September 23, September 30, October 7, 1937.

Ciano, Count Galeazzo, *Ciano's Diplomatic Papers*, London: Odhams Press Limited, 1948.

Ciano, Count Galeazzo, *Ciano's Hidden Diary*, trans. by Andreas Mayor, New York: E. P. Dutton and Co., 1953.

Craig, Gordon A., and Gilbert, Felex, *The Diplomats, 1919-1939*, New York: Princeton University Press, 1963.

Documents on German Foreign Policy, 1937, Washington: Dept. of State, 1964.

Fermi, Laura, *Mussolini*, Chicago: University of Chicago Press, 1961.

Hibbert, Christopher, *Il Duce*, Boston: Little, Brown and Co., 1962.

Hoffmann, Heinrich, *Mussolini Erlebt Deutschland*, Munich: Verlag Heinrich Hoffmann, 1937.

Illustrated London News, October 2, 1937.

Illustrirte Zeitung Leipzig, October 7, 1937.

Keesing's Contemporary Archives, 1937-1940, London: Keesing's Publ. Ltd.

Kirkpatrick, Ivane, *Mussolini—A Study in Power*, New York: Hawthorn Books, Inc., 1964.

Kirkpatrick, Ivane, *Mussolini—Study of a Demagogue*, London: Odhams Books Limited, 1964.

Life, October 18, 1937.

Macartney, Maxwell H. H., and Cremona, Paul, *Italy's Foreign and Colonial Policy, 1914-1937*, London: Oxford University Press, 1938.

Mussolini, Rachele, *My Life with Mussolini*, London: Robert Hale Limited, 1959.

Newsweek, October 4, 1937.

New York Times, September 24-30, 1937.

Schmidt, Paul, *Hitler's Interpreter*, London: Heinemann, 1951.

Shirer, William L., *Berlin Diary, 1934-41*, New York: Alfred A. Knopf, 1941.

Shirer, William L., *The Rise and Fall of the Third Reich*, New York: Simon and Schuster, 1960.

Time, October 4, October 11, 1937.

The Times (London), September 24-30, 1937.

OTHER R. JAMES BENDER PUBLICATIONS
    "AIR ORGANIZATIONS OF THE THIRD REICH"
    "ORDERS, DECORATIONS, MEDALS AND BADGES OF THE THIRD REICH"
    "UNIFORMS, ORGANIZATION AND HISTORY OF THE WAFFEN - SS"